BE COOL,
BE YOU

T0343540

BE COOL, BE YOU

Copyright © Summersdale Publishers Ltd, 2022

Poppy O'Neill has asserted her right to be identified as the author of this work in accordance with sections 77 and 78 of the Copyright, Designs and Patents Act 1988.

An Hachette UK Company
www.hachette.co.uk

Vie Books, an imprint of Summersdale Publishers Ltd
Part of Octopus Publishing Group Limited
Carmelite House
50 Victoria Embankment
LONDON
EC4Y 0DZ
UK

www.summersdale.com

Printed and bound in the UK by Bell & Bain Ltd, Glasgow

ISBN: 978-1-80007-339-5

Substantial discounts on bulk quantities of Summersdale books are available to corporations, professional associations and other organizations. For details contact general enquiries: telephone: +44 (0) 1243 771107 or email: enquiries@summersdale.com.

BE COOL, BE YOU

A Child's Guide to Making Friends

Poppy O'Neill

CONTENTS

FOREWORD

Amanda Ashman-Wymbs
Counsellor and Psychotherapist, registered and accredited by
the British Association for Counselling and Psychotherapy

Raising two girls and working therapeutically with children for many years has made it very clear to me that it is vital that our children learn how to develop confidence in their social skills, and how to understand and relate to themselves and others in caring and empathetic ways. Living in today's society is very demanding for children as they face the many challenges of growing up and the process of learning about themselves, others and the world around them. How they evolve in these ways has a strong impact on their relationships and well-being in childhood and adolescence and into adult life.

This friendly, interactive workbook by Poppy O'Neill is written in a way that helps the young reader to understand themselves and be kind to themselves and others, thus helping to develop self-confidence, compassion and empathy.

Throughout the text the child is supported in navigating the many values and challenges of their social interactions. The insights and exercises validate and normalize their feelings and experiences, and are offered in such a way that the child is able to identify the attributes of healthy and unhealthy friendships. They are given guidance in finding ways of managing and coping with these, as well as with the feelings that may arise in relation to them.

This is a much-needed book, which I highly recommend for helping a child to develop self-esteem and self-awareness as well as growing confidence in understanding and cultivating friendships in positive ways.

INTRODUCTION: A GUIDE FOR PARENTS AND CARERS

Be Cool, Be You is a guide that will support children as they navigate their social world, make friends and feel confident being themselves. Using activities and ideas inspired by techniques developed by child psychologists, this book will help your child understand the sometimes confusing and challenging world of friendships, find compassion for themselves and others, and learn to be their own best friend.

Developmental stages differ among children, but from around the ages of three or four they're able to begin to form friendships with their peers. For some, this will happen quite easily, but for others, social skills can be slower or more difficult to develop. It's important to point out here that struggling with friendships doesn't mean that there's something wrong. Some children (and adults) are happiest in their own company, and quality is certainly more important than quantity when it comes to friends. However, difficulty in forming close bonds with peers can be a source of great sadness and confusion.

Perhaps your child is having a hard time making friends, or shows signs of being unhappy in the friendships they do form. Maybe they seem to hide their true selves in order to be liked, or they've been affected by bullying in the past and feel anxious about forming new bonds. Making friends takes bravery and compromise, and that's why it's so important to nurture your child's self-esteem, so that they feel comfortable being themselves.

This book is for children aged 7–11, an age when social relationships start to come into their own. As their personalities develop, they're able to better discern who is and isn't a good fit for them. It's also an age when children become more conscious of what other people think of them. Coupled with the first signs of puberty and new pressures from school, it's no wonder some kids begin to find it difficult to connect with others. If this sounds like your child, you're not alone. With your support, patience and encouragement, they can build their confidence and social skills, enabling them to be themselves and form healthy friendships.

Signs that your child is struggling with friendships

Look out for signs such as these, as they may indicate that your child is having a hard time with friendships:

- They are often alone at break times

- They find it difficult to disagree or compromise

- They find it hard to follow rules

- They show very different personalities at home and at school

- They find it difficult to read social cues

- They say they don't want friends

- They are very shy

- They have been teased or bullied

It can be difficult to look in detail at our children's mental and emotional health – sometimes we, as parents and carers, might recognize painful aspects of our own younger selves, or ways in which our behaviour is unhelpful to our children. Be kind to yourself and remember you are only human. Friendships are complex, and there are no quick fixes, but taking an interest and supporting your child through challenges is the most tremendous gift.

How to use this book: For parents and carers

This book is for your child, so let them take the lead. Some children might be happy to work through the activities relatively independently, while others might want or need a little guidance and encouragement from you.

Even if your child wants to complete the activities alone, it's a good idea to show an interest and start a conversation about the book – anything they've learned or realized, any parts they've found confusing or helpful. A small way you can help your child to grow their social skills is by asking them their opinion!

The activities in *Be Cool, Be You* are designed to get your child thinking about the way their mind and emotions work, so reassure them that there are no wrong answers and they can go at their own pace. Hopefully, this book will help you both to gain a greater understanding of each other, as well as of how friendships work. However, if you have any serious concerns about your child's mental health, your doctor is the best person to turn to for advice.

HOW TO USE THIS BOOK: A GUIDE FOR CHILDREN

Do you ever find friendships tricky? Having friends is brilliant, but sometimes other people can be upsetting, annoying or downright confusing! The truth is, having friends is complicated because people are complicated, so finding it hard doesn't mean you're doing it wrong… it means you're doing it right.

Here are some of the most common difficulties that children your age deal with:

- Feeling like the odd one out

- Worrying you don't have enough friends

- Trying hard to fit in

- Finding it difficult to speak up for yourself

If that sounds like you, you're not alone! Lots of children feel this way and find friendships hard. This book is here to help you stand up for yourself, find good friends and be your brilliant self.

There are lots of activities and ideas to help you learn about how friendships, emotions and our minds work. You can go at your own pace, and you can get help from your grown-up at any time – there might be things in this book that you'd like to talk about with them, too. This book is for you and about you, so there are no wrong answers: you're the expert.

INTRODUCING BLIP THE MONSTER

Hi there! I'm Blip and I'm a friendly monster. I'll help guide you through this book – you'll see me here and there, so be sure to say hello when you do. Sometimes I find friendships tricky. If you do, too, that's OK: this book is here to help. It's packed with interesting ideas and fun activities – are you ready? Then let's get started.

PART 1:
FRIENDSHIP AND ME

In this chapter we're going to learn all about you, and all about friendship. Getting to know yourself is a really big part of being a good friend.

WHY ARE FRIENDSHIPS SOMETIMES TRICKY?

It's great to have friends – they're the people we love to see often and have the most fun with. We can be ourselves around our friends, and they're there for us when we feel down.

Because all human beings are unique, there are going to be times when you and your friends disagree with or upset each other. That doesn't mean there's something wrong – it means there's something right. Good friends can feel upset with each other and work it out.

Finding good pals can be hard, though! Sometimes it feels like we don't quite fit with the other children in the class, or the ones we'd like to be friends with don't notice us.

Friendships can be confusing, sometimes difficult… and lots of fun. With a bit of help, we can deal with the difficult bits, because the fun parts are worth it.

COMMON FRIENDSHIP STRUGGLES

What kind of things do children your age have to deal with when it comes to friendships? Here are just a few:

- Being left out or excluded

- Being bullied

- Friendships ending

- Moving to a new class or school

- Finding it difficult to play with others

- Being shy

- Worrying about not having enough friends

Perhaps one or more of these things has happened to you, or you worry about it happening. Or perhaps you're dealing with something that isn't on the list. Whatever worries or struggles you have, you're not alone – even if it feels that way sometimes.

ACTIVITY: ALL ABOUT ME

Let's get to know you better! Can you complete the sentences?

My name is...

I am __ years old.

Three words that describe me are...

I'm good at...

My favourite music is...

When I grow up I'd like to be...

ACTIVITY: MY FRIENDSHIPS

Have a think about the friendships you have: they can be children from school, family members and even pets!

Draw or write about your friends here:

What's it like being a friend?

*I'm a good friend when...*_____

_____

_____

_____.

*My favourite thing to do with a friend is...*_____

_____

_____

_____.

*I wish I had a friend who could...*_____

_____

_____

_____.

BEING A GOOD FRIEND

Being a good friend means being kind to others, but also being kind to yourself – and this can be difficult when you find friendships tricky. Here are some signs that you're having a hard time:

- You feel lonely

- You don't have much fun when you're with your friends

- Your friends are unkind to you

Being a friend takes a lot of courage – here are some signs that you're being a good, brave pal:

- You stick up for your friends if they're bullied

- You're kind to everyone you meet

- You don't do things just because everyone else is doing them

WHAT MAKES A GOOD FRIEND... AND A BAD ONE?

Not everyone is a good fit for friendship with you. Look out for these signs of good and bad friends:

A good friend...	A bad friend...
Talks to you kindly	Is mean to you
Lets you play with other friends	Tries to keep you to themselves
Cares about your feelings	Doesn't mind hurting your feelings
Is someone you feel calm around	Is someone you feel worried or scared around
Plays with you	Ignores you
Listens to you	Won't listen to you

- **If someone is behaving like a bad friend to you, remember that it's not your fault. You are in charge of your actions, and they are in charge of theirs. You don't have to be friends with someone who treats you badly. If you need help dealing with a bad friend, you can ask a trusted adult.**

WHO'S MY TRUSTED ADULT?

A trusted adult could be a parent, carer, teacher, neighbour, family member or someone else: they are grown-ups you feel comfortable talking to, who are good listeners and care about your feelings. You might have lots of adults in your life that you trust, or maybe just one or two. You don't need to trust someone just because they're an adult – trust is a feeling inside you.

Write or draw your trusted adult or adults here:

You can talk to them about anything that's worrying you.

ACTIVITY: FRIENDSHIP QUIZ

Take this quiz to find out what kind of friend you are!

1. **It's Monday morning and time to go to school. How do you feel?**
   a. I can't wait to see my friends
   b. I wish I could stay in bed – I hate school
   c. Getting up is so hard, but once I'm at school, my friends make it all worth it

2. **Your friend's been quiet all day, so you:**
   a. Tell jokes and do silly things to make them laugh
   b. Assume they're angry with you and avoid them
   c. Ask what's wrong and see if you can help them feel better

3. **I'm happiest...**
   a. With my friends
   b. By myself
   c. With my friends, but I also enjoy my own company

4. **There's a new child in class. You...**
   a. Make sure you're the first friend they make
   b. Ignore them – you have enough friends already
   c. Act friendly and welcoming – they could be a potential new friend

5. **Your BFF wants to sit with someone else at lunch. How do you feel?**
   a. Awful – I must have done something wrong
   b. Angry – we're no longer BFFs
   c. Relaxed – I'll miss them, but we'll catch up later

Mostly A: You care a lot about your friends and that makes you a wonderful person to be around. But sometimes you don't recognize how lucky your friends are to hang out with you. Remember to be a friend to yourself, too!

Mostly B: You're cautious about who you're friends with, and you worry about getting your feelings hurt. If friends have been unkind to you in the past, it's really understandable to feel worried! Learning how to trust someone enough to make friends with them is a brave thing to do.

Mostly C: You're a good friend to yourself and others – yay! You're not afraid to make mistakes and you feel relaxed, whether you're by yourself or with others. You're always excited to make a new friend and learn new friendship skills.

I CAN
DO MY
BEST

PART 2: KINDNESS

Being kind to yourself and to others is what makes friendships magic. In this chapter we'll explore why kindness is so important, as well as all the ways we can be kind to one another.

KINDNESS IS A SUPERPOWER

Showing kindness in big and small ways makes others feel better – that's a superpower that everybody has.

When you're kind to someone, it makes them feel good. But that's not all – the real magic is that it makes you feel good, too! When a person is kind to another person, both of their brains release serotonin and dopamine – amazing natural chemicals that make you feel positive.

How will you use your powers of kindness today?

ACTIVITY: I AM KIND

Kindness comes in lots of different forms! It can be helping a friend with a tricky question at school, getting help when someone is hurt or sharing yummy food.

Think of a time when you were kind to someone – write about or draw it here:

Now can you think of a time when someone was kind to you? Write about or draw it here:

Can you think of ways in which you're kind to yourself? Circle the ones that you spot below and add your own in the empty circles!

*I speak up when
I need help*

*I think kindly
about myself*

*When I'm
thirsty, I have
a drink*

*If I feel like
crying, I cry*

*When I feel cold, I
put on a sweater*

*When I'm
worried, I talk
about it*

*I do fun
things*

*I am a
good friend*

*I say no to things
I don't want to do*

ACTIVITY: ALL ABOUT EMOTIONS

Emotions are feelings we experience in our minds and bodies. Some examples of emotions are:

Happy

Sad

Scared

Relieved

Angry

Disgusted

Guilty

Disappointed

Worried

Jealous

Anxious

Embarrassed

Joyful

Excited

We feel emotions all over our bodies, and they have an effect on our thoughts and how we behave. Emotions are a part of being alive – all human beings and lots of animals feel them – and they are one of the ways we learn about the world. They're also a big part of friendship – read on to find out why.

WHAT IS EMPATHY?

Empathy means being able to know or imagine how someone else is feeling, even when you haven't had the same experience.

When you see things through another person's eyes, you have a better chance of working out how to show them kindness or offer help.

Let's give it a try:

Blip's beloved pet frog went missing last night.

How do you think Blip is feeling?

_____

_____

How could you show kindness to Blip?

_____

_____

Blip's frog is home!

How do you think Blip is feeling now?

_____

_____

How could you show kindness to Blip?

_____

_____

Excellent work: you used empathy!

EVERYONE IS DIFFERENT

Empathy is a brilliant skill, but you can only ever guess at how another person is feeling. It doesn't matter so much whether you're correct or not: it's about trying your best to imagine and show kindness.

Everyone has a unique set of experiences, feelings and ideas, so one situation might make two people feel very differently.

For example, the teacher announces that the class will be playing football instead of doing art in the afternoon.

Blip, who loves art, feels disappointed.

Fiz, who loves sport, feels excited.

Neither is right, or wrong – they just feel differently, and that's OK. We can use empathy to imagine what it's like for Blip and Fiz: we can feel happy for one and disappointed for the other at the same time.

It's also important to know that just because someone is feeling a difficult emotion – like disappointment – it doesn't mean we need to fix or change anything. Blip (and anyone else) is allowed to feel sad or angry. Just like Fiz (and anyone else) is allowed to feel happy and excited – and you are allowed to feel whichever emotions you feel.

WHAT IS SELF-TALK?

Self-talk is the way we speak to and about ourselves: it can be friendly or unfriendly, kind or unkind. You are the person you're with the most, so it's important to be a good friend to yourself, and not a bully.

The good news is, you have the power to change the way you speak to yourself and make it kinder. Just listening to your thoughts is the first step to growing a friendly self-talk voice.

Can you think of a time you thought or said something about yourself that was unkind? For example, "No one likes me because I fell over in the playground." If you like, you can write it down here:

Now imagine a friendlier self-talk voice. For example, "I felt embarrassed when I fell over – I wish it hadn't happened. I can ask a friend or trusted grown-up for a hug." Can you think of some kinder words you could have said to yourself instead?

ACTIVITY: WHAT IS BLIP FEELING?

Being able to recognize emotions is a big part of being a friend. When you can see, or guess, how someone is feeling, you know how to be a friend to them.
   Can you draw a line to match the Blip faces to the emotions?

Happy

Sad

Scared

Angry

Excited

Calm

ACTIVITY: FEELING LEFT OUT

Do you ever worry that other children don't like you? It's a common worry to have, so you're not alone. Our brains have evolved to think that fitting in with those around us is very important, so if we feel that we aren't liked or included within a friendship group, it can feel really uncomfortable.

It's OK to feel worries, and it's also important to remember that they aren't facts – they're just ideas and guesses that your brain is coming up with. You can show yourself kindness by thinking about hopeful ideas and guesses, too, like these:

I have good friends

I am a good friend

My friend is having a bad day – we are still friends

If your worried thoughts are upsetting, you can calm them by showing your brain some facts. Write your answers to the prompts below, and you can come back to this page next time you worry about being liked.

Someone who definitely likes me:

Something they have said or done that proves they like me:

SHOWING KINDNESS IN DIFFERENT WAYS

One of the reasons we get along with some people better than others is because everyone shows kindness in different ways. We all appreciate kindness, but some people like using words best, while others prefer hugs or high fives.

Here are some of the many ways we can show each other kindness. Draw a circle around the ways in which you like to show kindness.

Hugs

High fives

Encouragement

Asking about each other's day

Telling a joke

Sharing a snack

Drawing a portrait

Offering to help

Asking how we're feeling

Standing up for each other

Listening

Doing chores

Making lunch

Helping with
schoolwork

Reading
together

Giving gifts

Playing a
game together

Holding hands

Talking together

Writing
letters to
each other

Can you think of any more ways to show kindness?

I AM
A GOOD
FRIEND

ACTIVITY: HOW CAN MY FRIENDS SHOW ME KINDNESS?

Now, think about how you like friends to show you kindness. Write or draw your ideas here:

ACTIVITY: MAKE A KINDNESS POSTER

When you show kindness to yourself and others, it grows. Being kind makes people feel good, and when we feel good, we're kinder to ourselves and each other... like a kindness snowball getting bigger and bigger!

One way to spread kindness is by putting kind words on a poster and displaying it somewhere people can see them. Think about some kind words you'd like to spread to those around you – here are some ideas to get you started:

The world is full of kindness   *You are special*

Today is a good day   *Let's spread kindness*

You are cool   *Kindness is magical*

You can practise writing your kind message here, before putting it on your poster:

Write your kind words in the middle of the poster, then use pens, pencils or collage to make it really colourful.

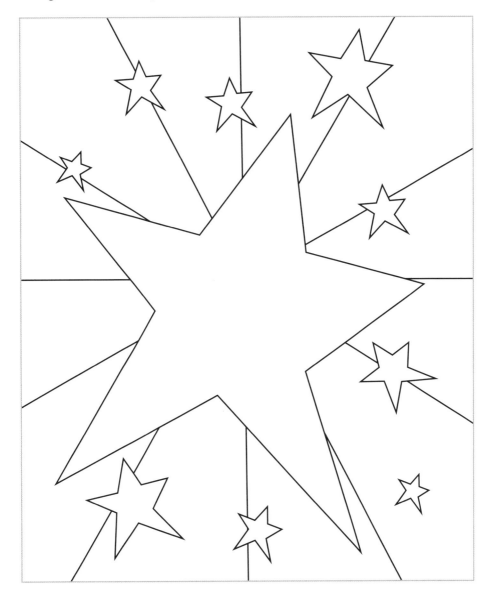

Be careful when cutting out this page

SHOWING RESPECT

There's something even more important than kindness, and that's respect. You don't need to be friends with someone in order to show them respect: it is something you can show to everyone you meet.

Respect means caring about how your words and actions impact others

Showing respect for others doesn't mean putting their feelings ahead of yours – it's about treating people the way you'd like them to treat you.

There's an important exception to this rule – if someone hurts you or makes you feel scared, you don't need to be respectful to them. Showing yourself respect means keeping yourself safe and talking to a trusted grown-up about what happened.

PART 3: MAKING FRIENDS

Making new friends can be tricky, and it takes a lot of courage to talk to new people. In this chapter you'll find lots of tips and fun ways to start up a new friendship.

WHAT ARE SOCIAL SKILLS?

Just like joined-up writing, riding a bike or tying your shoelaces, being a friend and getting along with others are skills that you learn. We call them "social skills" because "social" means being around other people.

Some people find social skills pretty easy, and they feel really comfy making friends and being around others. But for a lot of children and grown-ups, it's more difficult. It's OK if you find friendships hard or confusing. Learning about social skills can make them feel a bit easier and help you to get to know people, who might turn out to be a good fit for you.

WHAT DOES IT MEAN TO BE SENSITIVE?

If you're sensitive, you pick up lots of information and feelings that other people might not notice from the world around you. Flavours can taste stronger, noises sometimes sound louder and jokes might hurt your feelings more than they would another person. It's a bit like having the world turned up that bit louder, which can be annoying! This can make you feel shy or scared of meeting new people.

But sensitivity is an amazing thing to have, because it means that the world's more colourful, too. You have super-sensing powers that make you a brilliant friend with an interesting mind and a lot of kindness to give.

While sensitivity can mean that making friends feels extra tricky, it also gives you great social skills.

Sensitive people are brilliant at…

PRACTISE AT HOME

Practising socials skills at home will help you to feel more confident making friends when you're at school or out and about. Think of a situation you feel worried or nervous about, and ask a parent, carer or other trusted adult to act it out with you. Practising like this helps you to feel more confident about how you'd cope if the real thing happened.

Here are some ideas:

- Reading aloud in front of your class

- Asking someone to play

- What to do if you feel angry while at school

- Asking for help finding your way around

- Standing up to a bully

- Speaking up for yourself

You can act out the situation more than once, swap roles, make it funny, act out the worst outcome and the best… the more you practise, the easier it will be in real life.

ACTIVITY: RANDOM ACTS OF KINDNESS

A random act of kindness means showing kindness to someone without necessarily wanting to make friends with them. It's a great way to practise social skills, because you won't feel so nervous when you're not worried about whether the person wants to be friends with you or not.

Here are some random acts of kindness:

- Offering to help with chores at home

- Complimenting someone's outfit

- Holding the door open for the next person

- Letting someone go ahead of you in line

- Helping someone who's having trouble

- Hanging up someone's coat if it's fallen off the peg

- Writing a thank-you note

- Reading with someone younger than you

Can you think of any more examples?

The brilliant thing about random acts of kindness is that they make the other person feel good and they make you feel good, too! Showing kindness releases brain chemicals that bring you calm and happiness.

I AM
FUN!

GAMES TO PLAY

In the next few pages, you'll find a collection of different games to play with others. They've been picked because they can help you to get to know each other and build your confidence – and, above all, they're fun.

You can play these games almost anywhere, so next time you're getting to know someone new, or even spending time with an old friend or family member, try one out!

ACTIVITY: PAPER CREATURES

This game can be played with two or more players. It's a great way to make something funny and creative together.

You will need:

- Paper – an A4 sheet would work well

- Scissors (optional)

- Pencils or pens

How to play:

- Carefully cut or tear your paper into long strips, each about 5 cm (2 inches) wide.
- Draw a head at the top of one of the strips. Be as imaginative as possible!
- Fold the paper toward you, so your drawing is hidden – but the rest of the paper is not – and pass it to your friend.
- Your friend now draws a body, folds the paper and hands it back to you.
- Draw legs and feet (or tentacles, or rocket boosters!) and fold again.
- Open up the paper to see the amazing, mismatched creature you've created!

> **Tip: Have two strips of paper in play, so both players always have something to draw.**

ACTIVITY: LISTEN UP!

This game can be played in pairs and is perfect for learning to be an expert listener.

You will need:

⊛ Stopwatch or timer

How to play:

- Sit facing each other and set the stopwatch or timer for 30 seconds.
- One person speaks about a subject, while the other listens.
- When the time is up, the listener must try to repeat what the speaker said, as accurately as possible. The speaker can then tell them how well they remembered!
- Next, swap over so the listener has a turn speaking.

Ideas for subjects:
Pets, my dream house, the last film I watched, my favourite game, if I had a superpower it would be…

ACTIVITY: WOULD YOU RATHER?

This is a game for two or more people, and can be as interesting, funny, disgusting and exciting as you make it!

You will need:

- 🎗 Your imagination!

How to play:

- Take it in turns to ask each other interesting "Would you rather...?" questions. They can be yucky, funny, tricky or just plain silly – the point is to have fun and get to know each other better.
- Use the ideas below to get you started!

Would you rather be a bit too hot or a bit too cold?

Would you rather go bowling or swimming?

Would you rather be
friends or enemies
with a crocodile?

Would you rather
be able to fly or
to rewind time?

Would you rather
have a slug on your
eyebrow or an ant
up your nose?

Would you rather
eat only cake
forever or never
eat cake again?

ACTIVITY: MIRROR DRAWING

Be a copycat with this simple, creative game, which can be played in pairs.

You will need:

- A piece of paper

- Two pencils

How to play:

- Draw a line down the middle of the paper.
- Player one draws on one side of the line, while player two must draw the mirror image on the other side.
- Keep going until player two decides that the drawing is finished.
- Now turn over the paper and swap roles.

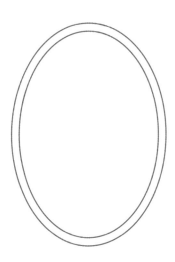

Try out mirror drawing with Blip!

Blip has drawn half a self-portrait on one side – can you make a mirror drawing?

ACTIVITY: SCAVENGER HUNT

Explore the world around you and collect up all the things on your list! This game can be played in person or on a video call.

You will need:

- A list of things to hunt (use Blip's lists on the next two pages or make up your own!)

- Pencil or pen

- Paper

How to play:

- Search in your home (or wherever you happen to be) for something to match every item on the list. Depending on the types of things, you can write them down or collect them. For example, if one of your objects is a sofa, you can write it down, but if another is a crayon, you can collect it.
- When you're ready, meet with the other players to share what you've found.

Outdoor scavenger hunt

- ☐ Something smooth
- ☐ Something rough
- ☐ Something fuzzy
- ☐ Something smaller than your thumbnail
- ☐ Something that looks like a face

At home scavenger hunt

- ☐ Something red
- ☐ Something orange
- ☐ Something yellow
- ☐ Something green
- ☐ Something blue
- ☐ Something purple

In town scavenger hunt

- ☐ Something that tells the time
- ☐ Someone wearing a uniform
- ☐ Someone wearing a hat
- ☐ Something that grows
- ☐ Something made of bricks
- ☐ A street sign
- ☐ Something older than you are

Video-call scavenger hunt

- ☐ A pair of clean socks
- ☐ A farm animal
- ☐ Something with its name on it
- ☐ One piece of toilet paper
- ☐ Something that has three different colours
- ☐ A picture of you
- ☐ Something with numbers on it

ACTIVITY: SQUARES

This game is quiet and relaxing, and works well with two people playing – make a bigger grid if you'd like to play for longer.

You will need:

- Dotted, squared or plain paper

- Pens or pencils in two different colours

How to play:

- If you're using plain paper, use a ruler to draw rows of dots about 5 mm (about a quarter of an inch) apart, until you have a grid of about ten dots going down and across.
- Take turns drawing a line between two dots.
- The aim is to be the one who completes a square. When you complete a square, write your initial inside it.
- When all the dots have been made into squares, the person with the most initials has won.

- **You'll notice this game has a winner – turn to page 94 to read more about winning and losing.**

You could practise playing squares with a grown-up. Here's a space for you to play:

ACTIVITY: CUT-OUT CONVERSATION CARDS

Sometimes it's hard to know what to talk about when you're getting to know someone, or even if you're already friends. Cut out and use these conversation cards to get you chatting; you can use them at home to build your conversation skills or memorize them, so you always have an interesting question ready.

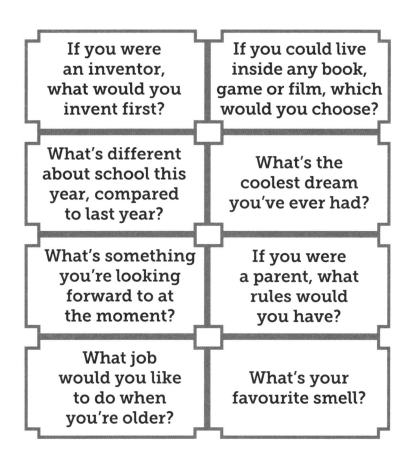

If you were an inventor, what would you invent first?

If you could live inside any book, game or film, which would you choose?

What's different about school this year, compared to last year?

What's the coolest dream you've ever had?

What's something you're looking forward to at the moment?

If you were a parent, what rules would you have?

What job would you like to do when you're older?

What's your favourite smell?

Be careful when cutting out this page

PART 4:
BEING A GOOD FRIEND

Having friends comes with all kinds of difficult bits, alongside the fun and lovely bits. If you and your friend disagree or fall out, that doesn't really mean there's anything wrong – it's a chance to work things out together and become even better at being a friend. In this chapter, we'll look at some of the trickiest parts of friendship, and how to deal with them.

BEING A GOOD FRIEND TO YOURSELF

When something tricky happens, and you or your friend are upset, it might feel like going along with what they want and making sure they feel OK is the best and kindest way to solve the problem. But it's important to be a good friend to yourself, too: how you feel matters just as much as how your friend feels. Finding a solution you're both happy with is more important than solving the problem quickly.

Being a good friend to yourself means speaking up for yourself, being honest about your feelings, and talking to and about yourself kindly. When you're a good friend to yourself, you can be a good friend to others, too.

I AM
IMPORTANT

ACTIVITY: PROBLEM-SOLVING

When there's a problem between friends, you can work together to find a solution. Blip is having trouble with his pal and has come up with three possible solutions, as well as a consequence for each:

Problem: My best friend is ignoring me!

Solution 1: ignore them back!

Solution 2: ask them what's wrong

Solution 3: play with someone else until they decide to talk to me again

Consequence 1: we might never speak again, but we'll be even

Consequence 2: they might say something I don't like... but at least I'll know

Consequence 3: I might not find out what was wrong, but it's up to them to tell me

Which solution would you choose? Draw a circle around it.
What made you pick that solution?

Now you try! Can you think of a problem? Perhaps it's something that's happened between you and a friend or sibling, or something you're worried about:

Can you think of three ways to deal with the situation?

1

2

3

What are the possible consequences for these solutions?

1

2

3

Which would you choose, and why?

ACTIVITY: ASKING FOR HELP

A lot of the time you'll be able to work out solutions to problems with your friends. But it's OK to ask for help from a grown-up whenever you need it.

When to try to work it out together

- When you both want a turn

- When you don't agree

- When someone is unkind

- When your friend wants to play with someone else

- When someone new wants to join your game

- When your friends are unkind about someone who isn't present

When to ask for help from a grown-up

- When you feel scared

- When someone is hurt

- When someone is unkind to you often

- When you or someone else is being bullied

- When someone asks you to keep a secret that doesn't feel good

- When someone takes or damages your things

- When someone asks you to do something you don't feel comfortable doing

- **Working out solutions together helps to build a stronger friendship and social skills. Asking for help from a grown-up when you need it is brave and the right thing to do!**

I STAND UP FOR MYSELF AND MY FRIENDS

ACTIVITY: BAD FRIENDS AND BULLIES

What's the difference between a bad friend and a bully? The main difference is that bullying makes you feel bad about yourself, and it happens over and over again.

Bullying is when someone tries to hurt you, scare you or make you do something you don't want to do, on a regular basis.

A good friend might say something unkind or act out when they're having a bad day, but they will put it right by saying sorry and they'll otherwise be kind to you.

Bullying can include:

Physical violence, like hitting or kicking

Name-calling

Pushing

Leaving you out

Stealing or damaging your things

Making you say things you don't believe

Making fun of you or your family

Imitating you

Ignoring you

Unwanted touching

Embarrassing you on purpose

Threats

Lying about you

Bullying can happen at school, on the internet or somewhere else. Anyone can be bullied, and it's always OK to ask for help if you are concerned or confused by the way someone is treating you.

SAY NO TO BULLYING

WHAT IS PEER PRESSURE?

Peer pressure is when your friends or other children you know make you feel like you should do, like or think exactly the same things as them.

Sometimes peer pressure can be about just wanting to fit in, but other times it can show itself when other children make fun of you for being different in some way. Both are difficult to stand up against, and it can feel hard to be yourself at times like these.

All my friends climb to the top of the climbing frame. They have fun up there, but I'm not ready yet – it seems too high and I don't feel comfortable.

Who's being a good friend to Blip? Draw a circle around the friend using peer pressure.

It's OK to walk away if you feel under pressure to do something that feels uncomfortable, even if lots of other people seem to be OK with it. You don't have to explain your reasons. Sometimes things just don't feel right.

PUTTING THINGS RIGHT

Even the best friendships have ups and downs. You might fall out with your friend, make a mistake, upset them or say something you didn't mean. You can do all of these things and still be a good friend – the key is that you put it right.

Friendships are like socks – if you get a hole in your favourite pair, you can either throw them away or you can repair them. Saying sorry and putting things right is like repairing the hole: it keeps your friendship going and even makes it stronger.

Blip and Bop went to a birthday party at the weekend. Blip left early without saying anything to Bop, who was upset and hurt – why would Blip leave the party like that?

Bop told Blip about these feelings, and asked why Blip had left. Blip apologized for hurting Bop's feelings.

I'm sorry I left without saying anything. It was too loud for me at the party, but I didn't think you'd understand.

I felt that, too! You being there made it feel less overwhelming.

Now Blip and Bop know each other even better, and next time they'll know it's best to talk about their feelings!

Putting things right doesn't always just mean saying the word "sorry". That is a powerful word, but it doesn't magically fix things – especially if you don't really feel sorry.

Putting things right with a friend can be:

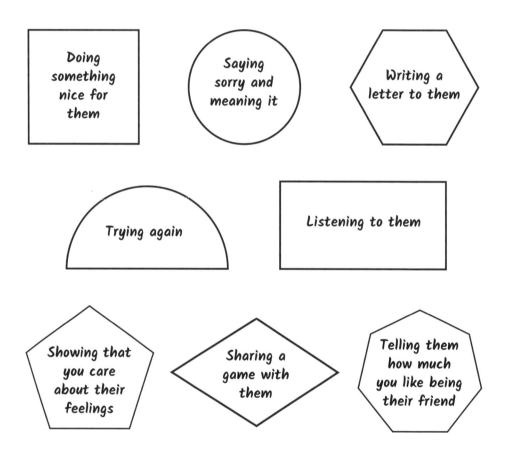

Doing something nice for them

Saying sorry and meaning it

Writing a letter to them

Trying again

Listening to them

Showing that you care about their feelings

Sharing a game with them

Telling them how much you like being their friend

ACTIVITY: FEELING ANGRY

Anger can be a really big emotion and when we're feeling big emotions, it's hard to be a good friend. Being angry can feel different for different people.

Write how anger feels for you in these speech bubbles:

When we feel anger, we feel it in our bodies. Can you draw how anger feels? You can use colours, patterns, words and shapes.

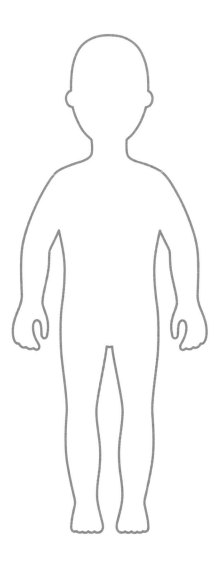

When you feel angry, there are things you can do that will help the feeling move through your body so you can feel calm again. Your angry feelings will pass, just like all feelings pass.

When I feel angry, I can…

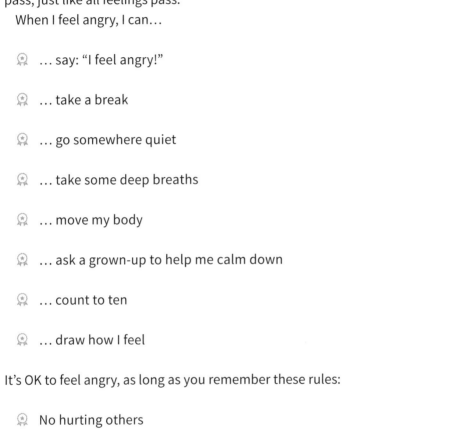

- … say: "I feel angry!"

- … take a break

- … go somewhere quiet

- … take some deep breaths

- … move my body

- … ask a grown-up to help me calm down

- … count to ten

- … draw how I feel

It's OK to feel angry, as long as you remember these rules:

- No hurting others

- No hurting yourself

- No damaging someone's property

ACTIVITY: FEELING JEALOUS

We feel jealous when someone else has something we think we deserve. Feeling jealous of a person can make you angry or upset at them – like if your friend has a new puppy, and you wish you had one, too.

Can you think of a time you felt jealous of a friend? Write or draw about it here:

Everyone feels jealous sometimes, and it's normal to feel jealous of your friends now and then. The best way to deal with this feeling is to turn it into a goal or hope. This doesn't mean it will come true quickly, but taking your jealous feelings and using them to learn about how you'd like your life to be will help you focus on something more positive.

Here's how:

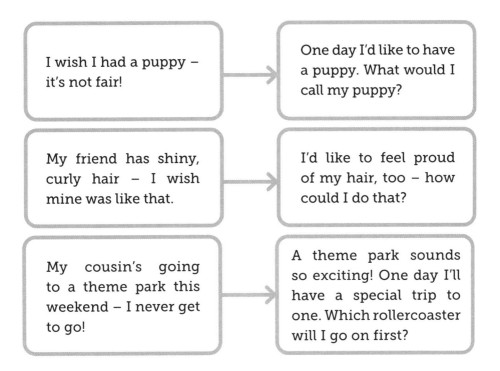

I wish I had a puppy – it's not fair!

One day I'd like to have a puppy. What would I call my puppy?

My friend has shiny, curly hair – I wish mine was like that.

I'd like to feel proud of my hair, too – how could I do that?

My cousin's going to a theme park this weekend – I never get to go!

A theme park sounds so exciting! One day I'll have a special trip to one. Which rollercoaster will I go on first?

- **When you feel jealous about something you can't change, look instead at how you think the person feels – what could you do to help yourself feel that way?**

WINNING AND LOSING

If winning, losing and following rules are tricky for you, it can take all the fun out of the games you play. It can also be frustrating when there are rules to follow. Perhaps you think rules make games less fun, or you feel angry when someone breaks the rules. Competitive games can bring up big feelings.

How does it feel to win a game?

Sometimes when we win, it's hard not to make others feel silly for losing. It's OK to enjoy winning, but try to treat others how you'd like to be treated.

How does it feel to lose a game?

Losing can make you feel embarrassed or angry, especially when you tried your best.

One way to help with big winning and losing feelings is to practise at home. Play games with your family – the best ones are those, like *Uno*, *Go Fish* or *Noughts and Crosses/Tic Tac Toe*, which are quick, so you have a chance to play again straight away. The more practice you get at winning, losing and following the rules, the easier it will be to deal with emotions and enjoy the game, whatever happens.

TAKING A BREAK

Big feelings can sometimes make us act in unfriendly ways. All emotions are OK, and it's also OK to express them – as long as you do it safely. Whenever a big feeling comes up – whether it's sadness about feeling left out, or pride from winning a game of *Go Fish* – taking a break will help you to feel calm and in control.

Here are some quick and easy ways to take a break. All of these will help to calm your body when you're feeling big emotions:

Take a deep breath

Get some fresh air

Find somewhere quiet

Count to ten

Do some star jumps

Read a book

Write in a journal or notebook

Draw a picture

Squeeze a teddy

Ask for a cuddle

Hum a song

Drum on your knees

YOU ARE AWESOME

You're doing so well! Some of the things written in this book might make you feel like you need to be different or change in some way, but that's not the case.

You are brilliant exactly as you are – the ideas in this book are here to help you be yourself *and* understand a little better how friendships work. Think of the suggestions in these pages as tools to help you build friendships where both you and your friends can be yourselves.

ACTIVITY: BELLY BREATHING

Taking a deep breath helps you to be a good friend because it helps you feel calmer and gives you a boost of confidence!

Belly breathing is a fun way to practise deep breathing and is a brilliant thing to do for:

- Relaxation

- Dealing with a big emotion

- An activity with a friend

Taking deep breaths calms your whole body, including your mind! It helps you to deal with big emotions, so you can be your brilliant self!

How to belly breathe:

- Grab something small and light – like a teddy, a book, a hat or a glove.

- Lie down flat on your back and place your object on your belly.

- Take a deep breath in through your nose, so the object moves up, and breathe out through your mouth, so it sinks down again.

- Try not to let the object fall off your belly!

BEING FRIENDLY AND BEING FRIENDS

You don't have to be friends with everyone – imagine how tiring that would be! But it's a good idea to be friendly to everyone you meet, which is different.
 Being friendly means:

- Being respectful
- Being polite
- Considering other people's feelings
- Being kind
- Being honest
- Being gentle

Being friendly does not mean:

- Playing with someone even though you don't want to
- Saying yes when you want to say no
- Always agreeing
- Accepting hugs you don't want
- Being unkind about yourself or others, because someone tells you to
- Keeping secrets that feel bad

I CAN TAKE
A DEEP BREATH

PART 5:
TAKING CARE OF YOU

Being a good friend to yourself means taking care of your body and mind. When your mind and body feel good, you become a great friend to others, too. In this chapter we'll find out about lots of different ways you can take brilliant care of yourself.

WHY IT'S IMPORTANT TO BE KIND TO YOURSELF

It's very difficult to be a good friend to others if you're not a good friend to yourself first. Notice how you think about yourself, especially when you've made a mistake or are feeling upset: the words you choose to use should be at least as kind as the ones you use for your friends – if not even kinder.

ACTIVITY: MY BEDTIME ROUTINE

Scientists – and probably parents, too – say that children your age should get about 10–11 hours' sleep every night. That's so your body can do all the growing it needs to, and you'll have enough energy to have fun and learn in the daytime.

But falling asleep can sometimes be really tricky. During the day, there are lots of things to do and be interested in, so your brain is kept busy with that. When it's time to go to sleep, your mind doesn't have all those interesting things, so it fills up with its own thoughts – interesting ones, scary ones… all sorts of thoughts.

So it's good to have relaxing things in your bedtime routine to help your mind switch off when it's time for sleeping, like:

Reading a book

Getting cosy in bed

Having cuddles with your grown-ups

Listening to a story

Cuddling soft toys

Turning off screens

Having a warm bath

What's your bedtime routine? Write or draw all the things you do in the evening before going to bed:

WONDERFUL WATER

Did you know that the human body is made up of about 60 per cent water? It's true! That's why drinking water is so important to feeling good and having plenty of energy.

Every time you sweat, go to the toilet, cry or breathe out, your body loses a little bit of water, so it's a good idea to have lots of drinks during the day. Just like a plant, you need to be topped up with water to stay healthy and energized.

Can you colour in the plant, giving it lush green leaves?

JUMP AROUND!

Moving your body is an important part of staying healthy. When you exercise, special feel-good chemicals are released by your brain, helping you to feel happier and more confident. There are loads of different types of exercise – what's your favourite?

_____

_____

Jumping is a fun, brilliant way to get your body moving. It gets your heart pumping – which makes it stronger and healthier – strengthens your bones and improves your sense of balance. You can jump with friends or by yourself – why not make it into a game, with music or stepping stones? Or just jump for the fun of it!

QUICK FRIENDSHIP MEDITATION

Meditation means sitting quietly, and calming your mind and body. It's a really lovely way to slow down and relax!

Find somewhere comfy and read this meditation slowly to yourself, or ask a grown-up to read it to you:

Imagine you are in a beautiful garden. You're warm and comfortable, and sitting on the grass. Look around – what else is in the garden? You can imagine anything you choose. Try to slow your breathing so you're taking long, deep breaths.

In front of you is a fountain with clear, sparkling water flowing from it. Can you hear the water babbling?

Imagine a coin in your hand. Think about dropping the coin into the fountain, and as you do, make a wish for yourself: may I be happy, may I be calm.

Another coin is in your hand now. Hear it plop as you drop it into the water, and make a wish for someone you love very much: may you be happy, may you be calm.

Keep plopping coins into the fountain, and wishing for happiness and calm. Each time you do it, think about a different friend, loved one or just someone you know: may you be happy, may you be calm.

Take a really deep breath in, and out. Your friendship meditation is finished.

- **This kind of meditation is called a "loving kindness" meditation. Invented by Buddhists, it helps to grow kind, friendly feelings for whoever you think of in your meditation.**

TALKING ABOUT FEELINGS

Everybody has feelings – they're a big part of what makes us who we are. Whatever you're feeling, being able to talk about it with someone you trust is an important part of taking care of yourself. Difficult emotions like anger and sadness can be hard to discuss, but sharing them with someone makes them easier to feel.

Who can you talk to about feelings? Think about who you trust and feel comfortable with. It might be a friend, brother or sister, parent or carer, a teacher or someone else.

Write or draw about them here:

ACTIVITY: FIND YOUR HAPPY PLACE

A happy place is somewhere you can go to, in your imagination, any time you like.

It could be somewhere cosy…

… somewhere wild…

… or wherever you feel happy!

What kind of happy place can you imagine? It could be somewhere you've been to, somewhere you've seen in a book or photo, or somewhere you've imagined.

Can you draw your own happy place? Add as much detail as you can!

Close your eyes and imagine you are in your happy place any time you want to relax, feel calm or need help with difficult emotions.

ACTIVITY: CALM COLOURING

Colouring helps you to feel calm, because your hands are busy with your pens or pencils, and your mind can enjoy the picture you create. Can you colour in these monster friends?

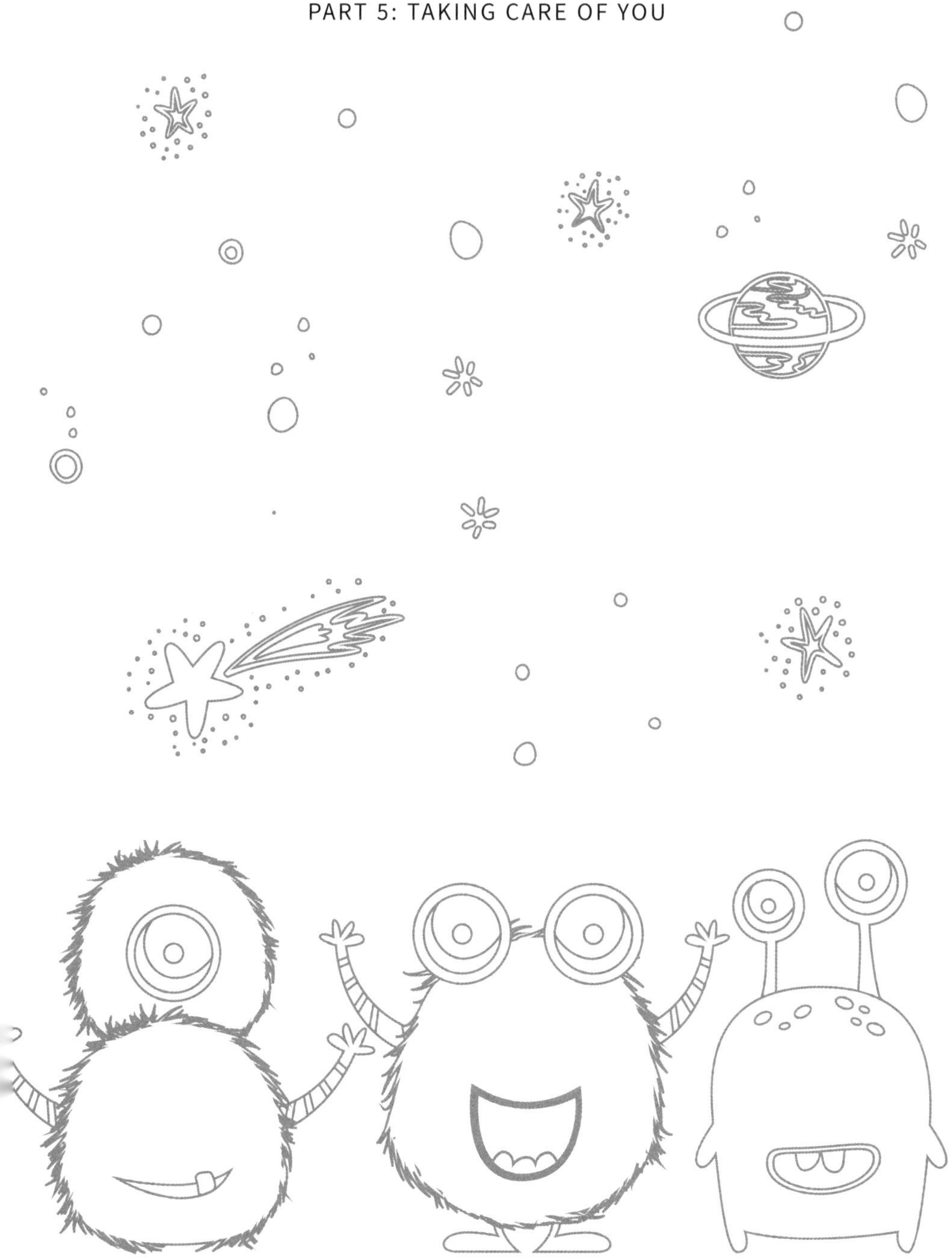

TAKING CARE OF YOUR FEELINGS

Everyone finds friendships difficult sometimes and feels hurt when they have an argument or are left out.

When you feel down about friendships, these tips will help:

- Talk about it. You don't need to keep your feelings a secret – talk to a trusted adult or another friend.

- Be kind to yourself. Just because one person isn't a good fit to be your friend doesn't mean you're not a brilliant, likeable person. Speak to yourself like you would speak to a good friend having a hard time.

- Chill out. Feeling upset or down is actually quite tiring! Take time to relax and do things you enjoy.

- Watch a funny movie. Pick one that makes you laugh every time – it'll lift your mood.

- Be brave. Remember that just because one thing didn't go your way, it doesn't mean you shouldn't try again.

ACTIVITY: A FUN SHARING RECIPE – CUCUMBER SUSHI

Cucumber sushi is a fun, healthy snack you can share with friends.

> - **Cucumber is packed with vitamins A, C, E and K, which help your body to stay healthy – plus, it boosts hydration!**

You will need:

- Knife
- Chopping board
- Spoon
- Bowl
- 2 cucumbers
- ½ red pepper
- ½ avocado
- 2 tablespoons sweetcorn
- ½ cup cooked and cooled rice
- Soy sauce to serve

Method:

1. Chop the cucumbers into rounds, about 2 cm (an inch) thick, and use a knife to remove the seeds, leaving doughnut-shaped pieces.
2. Chop the pepper and avocado into small cubes, then mix with the rice and sweetcorn in a bowl.
3. Use a tablespoon to stuff the rice and vegetable mixture into the hollow centres of the cucumbers. Use the bottom of the spoon to flatten the mixture.
4. Serve with soy sauce to dip.

IT'S GREAT BEING ME

PART 6:
LOOKING FORWARD

This is the last chapter of *Be Cool, Be You*! You're doing so well and should be very proud of yourself. In this chapter we'll look at all the things you've learned so far, as well as all the new tools and skills you can use in your friendships, today and in the future.

ACTIVITY: WHAT KIND OF FRIEND AM I?

Do you remember writing about what kind of friend you are in Part 1? Now that you've read all about friendships, what have you learned about yourself?

Draw yourself here, and add your top five friendship characteristics in the stars:

ACTIVITY: WHAT DO I LOOK FOR IN A FRIEND?

Have a think about what makes a good friend for you. Circle as many characteristics as you like!

Kind

Similar interests
to me

Funny

Clever

Honest

Energetic

Good listener

Good at
sharing

Big
imagination

Accepts me
as I am

Positive

Reliable

Cheerful

Helpful

Polite

Tidy

Chatty

Brave

Trustworthy

Enjoys computer games

Thoughtful

Enjoys sports

Enjoys reading

Takes turns

Confident

Artistic

Can you pick your top three characteristics of a good friend?

1 _____

2 _____

3 _____

ACTIVITY: MAKE A FRIENDSHIP GUIDE!

What's it like being friends with you? Make a friendship guide to find out! You could ask a friend to make one for themselves, too, so you can get to know each other better.

My favourite games...

My most fun toys...

I like to relax by...

A super-fun day would involve...

In the next year I'd like to play/learn/visit...

I DESERVE
TO SHINE

ACTIVITY: CAN YOU HELP BLIP?

Blip's friend Fiz is a fast runner – both Blip and Fiz have fun running around the field at school.

They both decide to join the running team – but there's only one place available.
   During the try-outs, Fiz slows down so that Blip can win the race and be chosen for the team.

Blip's really happy to be on the team, but knows that Fiz slowed down on purpose.
   Why do you think Fiz slowed down?

Was Fiz being a good friend to Blip?

Was Fiz being a good friend to Fiz?

Blip feels upset about what happened. What can Blip do to help make things right with Fiz?

WHAT TO DO IF YOU HAVE A BAD FRIEND

If someone you know is being unkind or treating you in a way you're not comfortable with, it's OK to speak up. Sometimes, the other person doesn't realize until you tell them how they are hurting your feelings.

If you explain and they're still not being a good friend to you, then you don't have to be their friend – even if they tell you you're being too sensitive, or that they are just joking. If it's difficult to get them to leave you alone, you can ask a trusted adult for help.

If you've been a bad friend:
We all make mistakes, and sometimes we hurt other people's feelings. If you've been unkind or a bad friend to someone, you can choose to be a good friend next time. Like we learned on page 87, saying sorry and making things right will grow strong friendships.

ACTIVITY: KEEP A JOURNAL

Journaling means writing about what goes on in your life, and how you feel about things. It's a great way to express your feelings and be creative – plus, it makes you feel calmer, too!

Try these journaling questions – there are no right or wrong answers!

Do you remember your first friend? What can you remember about them?

If there was a special day to celebrate friendship, what traditions would you choose for it?

What makes a friend a best friend?

If you and your friends formed a band, what kind of instruments would you play? What would your band be called?

- **You can use any notebook as a journal – why not write about your day as part of your bedtime routine?**

SPREAD FRIENDSHIP

When you show your friendship skills, you'll inspire others! Do you want to help other children grow great friendships? Here are six great ways:

- Welcome someone new into your game, especially if they're by themselves.

- Join a club (or start one!) Doing activities together is a great way to make friends.

- Use empathy. Imagine what it's like to be the other person, to understand them better.

- Show you care. Make cards or write notes to your friends, telling them how awesome they are.

- Ask for help. Parents, carers and teachers can help with friendship troubles, as well as organizing playdates or clubs!

- Be brave. Making new friends takes courage – be the brave one who talks to someone new.

STORIES OF FRIENDSHIP

Lots of children your age have friendship challenges – here are just a few of their stories:

At first, my best friend was really kind and we had a lot in common. But then she started saying mean things about the way I look. It really got me down, and she stopped feeling like a best friend... more like a bully. I started hanging out with a different group of friends and I don't really speak to her anymore.

Kara, 10

I'm homeschooled, so I have lots of different groups of friends rather than a class I see every day. Sometimes it feels weird being different to most children, but I get to do lots of interesting things and meet new people. I do have a best friend that I see most weeks at forest school.

Dylan, 8

My family moved to a new city this year, and I felt really shy, being the new kid at school and not knowing anyone. At first, I found it really hard to speak to the other children, but after a while I got to know everyone's name and found my way around the school, and it all felt a lot easier.

Evie, 11

I used to get really angry at school. Sitting still in a classroom was just so difficult and I'd get overwhelmed if anything went slightly wrong. I wasn't a very good friend because of it. My teachers helped me find ways to feel calmer, and it's really helped my friendships, too.

Jack, 10

I fell out with my best friend because her coat got ruined when she was at my house. I really missed playing with her, so I asked her if we could be friends again. She said yes and we make sure to wear old clothes for playing in my garden now.

Ali, 7

IT'S COOL
TO BE KIND

BE COOL, BE YOU
GOLDEN RULES

Be kind to yourself first

Show respect to
everyone you meet

It's OK to stand up
for yourself

You are brilliant,
just as you are

Be brave

Have fun!

ACTIVITY: ACTION PLAN

We've nearly reached the end of the book. Have you learned something that you'd like to use in your friendships?

_____

_____

A game I'll play…

_____

I'll take a break by…

_____

A good friend is…

_____

A bad friend is…

_____

I'd like to try…

_____

THE END

Blip's had a brilliant time learning all about friendship with you – have you enjoyed it, too? Remember: you can come back to this book any time you're having trouble with a friend, or need inspiration for making new ones.

You've done really well and should be very proud of yourself! Don't forget: you deserve great friendships, and you're cool exactly as you are.

For parents and carers: How to help children make friends

It's challenging to strike a balance between supporting your child in their friendships and allowing their independence to grow. You know your child better than anyone and you can trust yourself to get that balance right. Even if you make a mistake, you can learn valuable lessons that will help you along the way.

The most powerful way you can influence your child is by listening to them, showing an interest in their ideas and encouraging them to be themselves. Support them to express their emotions in healthy ways and show them how to treat others with respect – they'll learn from what you do far more than what you say.

There's certainly no one-size-fits-all blueprint for friendships, and your child will surprise and challenge you again and again with their ever-evolving personality. By taking an interest in their social development and guiding them toward a greater understanding of the way we build good relationships, you're giving them the best chance to grow into a strong, resilient adult who is capable of being a good friend to themselves and others.

While friendships between younger children are relatively straightforward, around this age they can become more complex. Peer pressure, hormones and an increased awareness of how we're perceived by others can lead to fallouts and unkind behaviour. Supporting your child emotionally will help to give them the resilience needed to weather any friendship storm. Show them every day that you value their uniqueness, that it's OK to feel different and it's OK to find things difficult.

I hope this book has been helpful for you and your child – always remember that they are not alone, and neither are you. There are so many wonderful friendships just waiting to be discovered.

Further advice

If you're worried about your child's mental health, do talk it through with your doctor. While almost all children will experience difficulties with friendships and social situations, some may benefit from extra help. There are lots of great resources out there for information and guidance on children's mental health:

YoungMinds Parents' Helpline (UK)
www.youngminds.org.uk
0808 802 5544

BBC Bitesize (UK)
www.bbc.co.uk/bitesize/support

Childline (UK)
www.childline.org.uk
0800 1111

Child Mind Institute (USA)
www.childmind.org

The Youth Mental Health Project (USA)
www.ymhproject.org

UK Council for Psychotherapy
www.psychotherapy.org.uk

British Association for Counselling and Psychotherapy
www.bacp.co.uk

Recommended reading

The Friendship Maze: How to Help Your Child Navigate Their Way to Positive and Happier Friendships by Tanith Carey
Vie, 2019

Stand Up for Yourself & Your Friends: Dealing With Bullies & Bossiness and Finding a Better Way by Patti Kelley Criswell
American Girl Publishing Inc, 2016

The Story Cure: An A–Z of Books to Keep Children Happy, Healthy and Wise by Ella Berthoud and Susan Elderkin
Canongate Books, 2016

The Floor Is Lava: and 99 More Games for Everyone, Everywhere by Ivan Brett
Headline Home, 2018

Credits

pp.13, 14, 15, 28, 32, 33, 34, 35, 36, 39, 48, 50, 51, 52, 53, 55, 56, 74, 75, 76, 78, 80, 81, 85, 86, 87, 92, 96, 103, 104, 105, 110, 111, 116, 123, 124, 136 – monsters © mers1na/Shutterstock.com; p.14 – mirror © ShutterLibrary/Shutterstock.com; p.20 – boy and girl © hasiru/Shutterstock.com; p.28 – food © davooda/Shutterstock.com; p.29 – superhero © mijatmijatovic/Shutterstock.com; pp.33, 39 – thought bubble © Paket/Shutterstock.com; pp.33, 34 – frog © Angyee Patipat/Shutterstock.com; p.35 – palette and brushes © Alexander_P/Shutterstock.com; p.36 – football © dimensi_design/Shutterstock.com; p.39 – emoticons © SpicyTruffel/Shutterstock.com; p.51 – flower © Evgeniia Andronova/Shutterstock.com; p.60 – children noughts and crosses © mijatmijatovic/Shutterstock.com; p.63 – bowling pins © Miceking/Shutterstock.com; p.64 – crocodile © Tanmoy Datto/Shutterstock.com; p.64 – cake © suesse/Shutterstock.com; pp.68, 69 – notepaper © Forgem/Shutterstock.com; p.85 – climbing frame © vectorchef/Shutterstock.com; p.88 – shapes © wilkastok/Shutterstock.com; pp.48, 50, 55, 56, 63, 64, 75, 85, 86, 87, 89, 101 – speech bubbles © Paket/Shutterstock.com; p.90 – body outline © Anna Rassadnikova/Shutterstock.com; p.92 – puppy © Alona Savchuk/Shutterstock.com; p.96 – building blocks © Jamila Aliyeva/Shutterstock.com; p.100 – healthy children © mijatmijatovic/Shutterstock.com; p.102 – bath © nadiia_oborska/Shutterstock.com; pp.102, 103 – teddy © IrynMerry/Shutterstock.com; p.102 – book © Puckung/Shutterstock.com; p.104 – watering can © Lidiia Koval/Shutterstock.com; p.105 – plant © Lena L/Shutterstock.com; p.108 – bedroom © nadiia_oborska/Shutterstock.com; p.108 – forest © Aluna1/Shutterstock.com; p.108 – spaceship © AllNikArt/Shutterstock.com; p.116 – mountain © Barmaleeva/Shutterstock.com; p.117 – stars © andvasiliev/Shutterstock.com; p.124 – trophy © ERRER/Shutterstock.com; p.128 – children skipping © mijatmijatovic/Shutterstock.com; p.129 – children on seesaw © mijatmijatovic/Shutterstock.com; p.134 – scroll © MasterGraph/Shutterstock.com; p.136 – streamers © dimair/Shutterstock.com

Other Vie books for parents, carers and children...

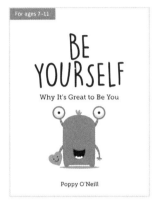

£10.99

Paperback

ISBN: 978-1-78783-608-2

£10.99

Paperback

ISBN: 978-1-78685-236-6

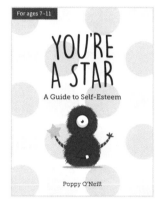

£10.99

Paperback

ISBN: 978-1-78685-235-9

£10.99

Paperback

ISBN: 978-1-78783-607-5

£10.99

Paperback

ISBN: 978-1-80007-340-1

£10.99

Paperback

ISBN: 978-1-78783-699-0

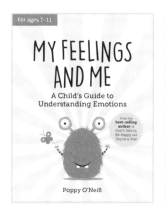

£10.99
Paperback
ISBN: 978-1-80007-338-8

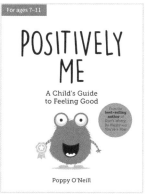

£10.99
Paperback
ISBN: 978-1-80007-169-8

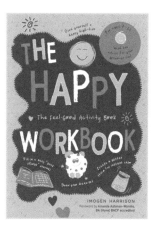

£10.99
Paperback
ISBN: 978-1-78783-990-8

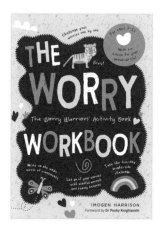

£10.99
Paperback
ISBN: 978-1-78783-537-5

£10.99
Paperback
ISBN: 978-1-80007-337-1

£10.99
Paperback
ISBN: 978-1-80007-168-1

Have you enjoyed this book?
If so, why not write a review on your favourite website?

If you're interested in finding out more about our books,
find us on Facebook at **Summersdale Publishers**, on Twitter
at **@Summersdale** and on Instagram at **@summersdalebooks**
and get in touch. We'd love to hear from you!

Thanks very much for buying this Summersdale book.

www.summersdale.com